Thinking Out Loud

Thinking Out Loud

AARUSHE SHARMA

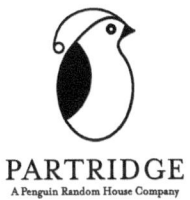

PARTRIDGE
A Penguin Random House Company

ISBN: Softcover   978-1-4828-5676-7
                eBook   978-1-4828-5677-4

Because of the dynamic nature of the Internet, any web addresses or links contained in this book may have changed since publication and may no longer be valid. The views expressed in this work are solely those of the author and do not necessarily reflect the views of the publisher, and the publisher hereby disclaims any responsibility for them.

Print information available on the last page.

To order additional copies of this book, contact
Partridge India
000 800 10062 62
orders.india@partridgepublishing.com

www.partridgepublishing.com/india

CONTENTS

for those who are lost in their attempts to let go.

ACKNOWLEDGEMENT

For their encouragement in getting me to publish my script, I would like to express immense gratitude to my grandparents and parents, who helped me without asking for it.

To Cheryl, for being the innocent little sister that she is.

To Nitesh Rai, the batch mate and friend for consistently supporting me through writer's block.

The people I live with and the ones I do not but anyways love.

People

Words are not for ignorant people, for the ones who let it be,
they are for people who feel the core of their existence,
who understand the flip side of life,
who feel strong and listen close.
They are for people who feel the desire to express everything they feel with the seemingly heavy words and difficult sounds.
People who do not believe in small talk.
People who do not believe in getting their emotions go.

People who believe in deepened and strengthened expressions. They are not for someone who cuts out on coming out in the open.

So, my love, the masks you wear and the inhibitions you let cover your mind are destroying you to no limits.

I believe that even though you must have a hundreds of roles to play to the few people in your life, you can sustain and live with the deepest truth of your consciousness and identities.

You can still be the person only you know you are deep down.

Not everybody is going to love your work. There are going to be people who will not appreciate it - be it out of prejudices, out of negative emotions or may be just because they have the right to choose what they like.

Here, we all need to meet people who are broken - not for us, but for them.
People who have been there, pulling their insides off and keeping them out to the people they have loved the most.
People who have battled what does not show.
People who have tangled and untangled day in and day out within the complexities of the sense of feeling.

People who have survived the inabilities of being understood to be an average soul.
Souls that have been able to survive just as more averagely as most humans do.

Here, we all need to see people who are broken yet settled - not for them, but for us.

They are just not going to chase you for things they do not value. It is only some of them who would do that.

Only a few who would love you no matter what.

I wonder if it is as difficult for others to go on taking their lives ahead like it becomes for me. Do they stop at the thought of a possible breakdown?
Do they pay heed to the truth that they all need some more love?

I guess it rarely happens that a writer writes when he feels like writing.
He writes when his soul feels like talking.

Ever realized how similar we are in our hopes and in our shortcomings, in our endeavours and in the things we love?

You see a smile?
It hides a hundred faces.
Several lies.
Numerous dreams.
Each one of the ones you see.
It comes forward crossing paths of tumultuous thoughts. Stressing upon going back to its cradle upon every little detail that reminds it of its pain.

Life is a dirty trick played on us.
And those who are hung up on the thought of staying immortal in the memoirs of history won't break through it.

It is strange how hardships create the different kind of people that we are.
They break some of us, but then they make most of us.

We all grow and turn into someone we do not know of.

In your life, you are going to cross paths with people who will be the exact opposites of your identity.
Their ideology would be as strange to you as yours would be to them.
But then there may be a trick, a twist of faith, they may be the closest people you have in your life, they could be the closest you have been to a person.

In either case, you won't have to fight them or the reality that they are a crucial part of your life.

You will have to accept them, just the way they are.

Fighting them won't help.

Changing them won't help either, in fact, you can never change a person.

You may disagree on every decision that needs to be taken.

You may feel suffocated doing things you never thought you would do for another soul.

The biggest mistake a writer does is letting his thoughts be.

People owe you nothing.

It is all maybe a pre planned trap that you cross paths

and your lives entangle. It is maybe because of the trap that the very same people create a beautiful mess for you and them to sort together.

People owe you nothing, it is always more of a privilege than an obligation when someone sets everything aside and pays attention to you.

There is a different kind of aura hard working people have.
People who have worked their souls out in the past.
People who have been there for others.
People who have did it all because they love the ones they hold close.

It is weird how we criticize the good that is bestowed upon us and unknowingly accept the bad because that is what we think we deserve.

There are some kinds of people you meet.
You cross paths with them.
You have your destiny, your life, your story intertwined with that of theirs.
They are probably responsible for transforming your life to a certain extent.
They may help you achieve the goals you have been trying to achieve since ever.
They may help you mould yourself.

People do not always see how beautiful they are. They do not always see how perfect they are in what they are passionate about.

It is the intensity that makes it so.

The desire that grows up to be so immune that nothing remains alive under its touch.

You cannot make people stay if they do not want to.

All you can do is silently wish them to realize how much you did for them and how much you would still do for them.

The good news is - they always realize.

People are creatures full of flaws.

You cannot always bet on their judgment, but you can love them inspite of their flaws.

The days were spent with people,
And the night, with pills.
The days were enjoyed by the people,
And the night, with heart wrenching stills.

It is not wrong to drop the toxic people out of your life but sometimes you wait for their colours to fade.

Far away from the land of people,
from the roots of attachment,

and the sources of deceit - that is where I want to be.

We are all so used to feeling like people owe something to us that we forgo the truth that this life is ours to live.
It is our own failures and our beliefs we need to taste.
Our own dreams we need to live. Our own wishes we need to wish on stars.

There are damaged people who have been through things made to happen by others that words cannot explain.
And then there are exploited people, crushed and shattered by their own expectations,

their own failures and sometimes their own dreams.

The day you start believing that the most wonderful people you know of started from where you are, you know, it is attainable.

There are people who are mostly right.
 Not in the grand endeavours of their lives, but in the day-to-day things.
 In things like forgiveness and trying, in ventures of letting go, in their attempts to know.

Some people are just not the answer.
Stop questioning them.
Some things we crave to hear never come to us.

Never let the people from your past control any side of you.
Never let them be the reason you give up today.

It is only the cautious trying to be aware.
The fearless taking up everything.
The loved ones loving everybody.
The inclined ones following it with their heart and soul.

The heartless ones going along with the cold depths of an unemotional life.

Maybe it is not the place they come from,
maybe it is the kind of soul that they are.

We are more or less confined to the suitable perspectives of only what we see, what we feel and where we are.

You may never get the chance to get there. You may be too blessed to reach a position where betrayal knocks you down.

But that does not mean that you won't have the chance to heal another soul.

It indeed would be a boon.

To make someone smile.

To help them bring all their broken pieces back together.

Do not miss the chance to heal them.

You may or may not be able to make their wounds vanish entirely, but in the process, you will learn something of utmost value.

You will learn that you were given this life because there are purposes to be achieved by you - purposes that require you to work selflessly.

Targets that no other soul could ever achieve as effortlessly as you could,

because that is what you were
made for,
because it requires a soul just
like you.

You may not be aware but there
are always hundreds of people
linked to your existence at any
given moment.
You have to take a closer look
at it.
Your destiny is entwined with
them.
You may have no idea how you
need them.
You may not even be aware
that you do, but every single
person that contributes to
your identity is crucial to you.

Maybe just stop doing what you are doing right now.
Look around,
They won't stay for long,
They may leave without a single sound,
but then why should it matter?
We have been told, in this world, it is only the one who is wounded who gets to be crowned.

Why make someone live under the pressure of your presence?
Why not just let them be themselves, because that is the closest to perfect that they can be.

Hardships sometimes make you realize how much you need others to survive.

How easily we forget that karma always prevails; how easily we forget the fundamental truths of life while dealing with others.

The average mind does its deal for the burden of truth.

It is just illusions we leave behind.

Half of the things they say and are believed by us is because we just think they know.

Even if our plan of life is entirely different from theirs, we just believe them.
Just because they have been there already.

As if life is that predictable.

Nothing looks better than a soul drenched deep within its passion,
trying to hit the right chords.

There is little you can do to make someone happy if you are not their source of happiness.

If I was to die, I would let you hold me and touch me to my finest core,
And maybe then would it be when we will realize why it all begins when some things end.

The people who live up to the expectations of their souls, the ones who listen to their conscience more than their rationally drunk brains, the ones who give up on rationale but never on their hearts.

Sometimes, when we find logic while we simplify - we lose the value, we lose the beauty.

We all have a plan for life.
It has already been made.

And mind you, it is nowhere even close to the one we see it to be.
And only the ones who care to look beyond the routine endeavours will get to skip to the grounds marked for them.

Some become your universe, while others, strangely seem to be a grain of nothingness.

All of them do not love you.
Maybe the idea of you.
Maybe the idea of loving you, but not you.

LOVE

You are no different from the
alcohol that enters my veins.
Just as bitter,
Just as satisfying.

With no exceptions, I always
fall back with you,
fall back to you.

We adamantly hold our heart
closest to us so that it is not
hurt by another soul, but when
it comes to loving our soul, we
follow our minds.

Distances are merely spaces that yearn to meet like we do.
Places that go on singing of their virtues.
Places that urge to dwell into one another and let go of everything else when the right time comes.

Sometimes she wakes up in the middle of the night, drowned in the memory of what she dreads.

It hurts to be away from your identity, to be away from who you are and live being someone lost who does not seem to be able to put an end to the search.

In a perpetual search of a potion that lets her forget what she is made to live with and live with what she is all about.

There are very few people to keep close to ourselves for our entire lives and to make it easier for us, every now and then they keep on proving it to us.

You are the pain that life inflicts on me,
The irony I am asked to deal with,
The essence I never asked for,
The joy I never knew existed.

Have you ever been so engrossed with something that you feel you have been leaving your own trails behind, like you have been literally leaving yourself behind?
When it becomes all you can think of.
And it takes your time, your effort and a lot of your mind.
When it becomes what you sleep on and what you sleep with.
When nothing feels better than being good at it.

Well, that's sick!

My fears have been coloured the same way as yours,
We might as well create a masterpiece from the tainted scars.

I know we could fall apart,
and like other people who
seem to know what the future
holds and who seem to know
they are going to be together
forever,
I would rather keep it this way,
for it makes me work for you.
The thought of losing you
makes me try.
I would rather be afraid to lose
you and work for it than think
that you are here to stay and
let things be.

You stay here,
Just stay here,
And I will let you be,
But when it comes to our
differing dreams,
You might want to leave.

I would want to melt and let
go of the residues,
The way intoxication does it,
And speak no word until it
becomes clear to me how
feelings function.

It breaks my heart to know
that one day there will not be
a tomorrow.
A tomorrow for us to right our
wrongs.
There will not be a tomorrow
for you to get it back to how it
used to be and for me to say
things I always feel.

I wonder what would have
happened if I would have let
the feeling be and not tried to
have you,

What would have happened
if I had not made myself to
realize what I had was worth
thinking upon.

He is more like the Augusts to
my heat.
Filling me up till I defeat
So unless I fall,
it does not pour,
But then he still proves to be
the cure.

And then I have moments
when I realize how peaceful I
was without you.
Unloved but peaceful.

And I would want you to take
me from a horizon of being

loved so much to someone difficult to love so that it is just you and no one else who knows of the treasures I possess.

The moon would certainly lose its beauty if not found to be imperfect - just the way a soul loses the hope of being loved if perfect.

It is nice how you do it.
How you try to let go of the words you had once spoken.
How you believe that some things end where they end and nothing new grows.
How you believe that nothing stems out of hope.

It feels ridiculous knowing that I have you today, knowing that each and every bits and pieces of your existence fall close to mine. Seeing you love me in a way no other soul would dare to.

Feeling you treasure me for a place that I have never been to. It feels so ridiculous knowing that I have you today and realizing you could be out on your search for someone else tomorrow.

I love people I randomly see across the streets, when they eventually appear - pass a delightful smile to you for no known reason.

You smile back at them.

You return them the bundle of joy they just came up to you with - and they leave.
They leave you with a state of mind with a higher degree of peace than before.

There is something strange about the people you love.
They possess a certain magic and the magic works when you accept them with all their flaws.

Well, my love, there is no proof of ill will. You cannot just judge an individual's love for his deeds through his actions.

It takes soul to love something as intensely as we love our own selves.

Make sure you do not make them regret the choices they have made when someone chooses to open up to you.

The truth is that in the end, nobody is going to stay.
You will have to deal with your demons on your own.
You will have to convince yourself that even though your people love you like anything, they cannot fight your wars for you, they cannot step on to your battlefields.

Love is one of those things that have the potential to make you believe that life is not what ceases to continue, it is us, who cease to move ahead.

Maybe it was your love that kept me going,
maybe it was your hatred that kept me searching.

The beginnings are going to be beautiful.
The end?
Oh love, there is going to be no end.
That is, only if you remember one thing - they are human.
They have the tendency and the right to commit mistakes.
They love you nonetheless.
They are not biased yet.

They will do blunders, break your heart every once in a while and come back to you again and again - seeking your love.
Just do not forget they can and possibly are going to be wrong. Well, at times.
The rest of the times, I promise you would be able to manage and sail beneath the waves of their love.

Now that you are gone, every essence of your existence ceases to go away.
Every grain of your beauty stays like it is mine to bear.
The very colour of your dreams haunts me,
And it has all turned into a life that's hard to complete.

So maybe it was there already,
All planned,
Maybe you do not have to worry about things you think of all the time.
Maybe all you need to do is love and be loved.
Maybe you just have to be lovable.

Let your belongings be all about the things you love.
Let your possessions speak of the horizons of your love's intensity for things alike.

Would it bring you any relief if I said you no longer had to love me in spite of my flaws?

There is always a scope.
Scope for hope.
Scope for a better love to be found.
And that is what hurts.

The circle of life merely makes a difference. Souls that love each other remain the same, remain together.

They had a parallel universe.
They had parallel understanding of things.
They were too different.
They both never knew how it was to be with someone like the other.
None of them wanted to.

You do not see the road that leads to a love that knows no bounds and has no roots.
Nor is it so that you can catch the skies and behold what happens until you give in to such a love.

His love was not the usual kind.
It was the type that awoke at the midnight hour of a lonely night,
The type that awakens the soul amidst a perpetual journey.
And the kind that was not everyone's cup of tea.

Maybe it is us who simplify things just so that it becomes easier for them to love us.

Maybe we simplify ourselves
so that we begin to understand
what we are about.
And perhaps we forget to do
the same to others so that it
becomes easier for us to love
them.
Why not?
We are all the same at the end
of the day.

It is what we attach beings
with,
How we feel when their name
I taken,
How our heart beats an extra
beat,
How we label them to be our
sorrow and our joy.

We all see the ones we love
the most to be the most purest

souls, betraying their flaws, overlooking their failures.

If that is how it works, aren't we all perfect already?

What other perfection do we need than to be able to become someone who is dearly loved by another, here in this world?

Not everybody says "I love you" to tell you that they do.

Some prefer to make you feel protective,

Some skip their preferences for you,

Some need you to take care of yourself,

And some only want you to be true.

I hope the small things you do and the huge initiatives you take bring you to the desired place.

I hope people never fail to understand the pain you go through.

I hope what life gives you is just what you ask for.

You do not have the eyes to see how beautiful your soul is to me.

But then there used to be nights where even the faintest of smoke on the window pane brought back the memories of a clichéd yet eternal bond.

Emotions are one heck of a trouble.
They bind you into something that, after a certain time, becomes un-doable.
And twist your perspective.
And create a lump in your throat that becomes as inevitable as you would think of it to be.

Hide behind a million faces, you would still not know if it is gone,
come out in the open some day.
It is not as bad as it burns.

'' I think it is gross to let someone have a part of you, you know you need'', he said, ''even pathetic when you know that it is never coming back to you."

The quilts were off and the pride was shown - no one could ever really belong there.

You would really have to stay to see what your aura does to me. It is more or less like a circle of life and tough - when it reaches to a point of being defined.

Sometimes it so happens that I forget to let go of you, not even if it comforts me.

Bring me your pain,
I will keep it with me.

So you can go ahead and
spend the nights with glee.

I do not think I need anybody.
My mind has enough
contradictions of its own to
get someone along and fight
theirs too.

Do not ever forget that those
moments of interaction are
different from the moments of
intimacy, the silent promises
and the bond that smoothens
with every step.

If I never see you again, just so
you know,

You will always stay in the corners of my heart, covered with shades of hope.
And you may find pain,

The way he laughs, it seems like a child growing out of a seemingly sensible being.
Like life blooming out of a pretentiously captured soul and it does not take long for one to see how beautiful it is to have someone smile like they owe nothing to the world.
To see that sometimes what you see is the real version.

The vulnerabilities were kept open already.
Wounds stretched to limits.

Pain scraped off through depths.
What really then remains to hide.

I want to be the one who touches your soul and rips your fears off, replacing shattered pieces of hope with courage and broken dreams with grains of possibilities.

If relationships never die a natural death, are they meant to be forever?

Because sometimes we do not see how much of effort it takes

for a soul to do something for us, how comfortable it all looks to us and how difficult it actually is for them.

Let's stay quiet, look at each other, and find again what made us lose ourselves.

Cry all I want and you still won't get back, it is a cobweb of emotions that I do not know how to track.

The road that leads to a love that knows no bounds but has no roots.

Nor is it so that you can catch the skies and behold what happens until you give in.

It is only when I come back home to your arms that I can breathe away the poison and swallow the sweet truth of your presence knowing that you would stay and make me feel home while I go out to the world and fight my battles with reality.

When you love someone selflessly, you have nothing to lose. A part of everything they are stays in you. A part of everything you choose stems from them.

There are times I cannot express how is it that I feel so much for you. There are times when that is all I want to know.

So whenever silence takes over, it dawns upon my mind if you feel the same.
And even if there are things that bother you, you may just close your eyes and let me help, I will take you to the stars that shine endlessly in your imagination.
I will take you to places that are mirrors of the warmth you have and yet cannot compete.

I want you to look deep into my eyes and tell me what you

see beneath the failures I have
let go off.
What possibilities do you
sense for the moments that are
yet to come,
what fears do you see growing
in the dark graveyards of my
heart.

You do not see yourself the
way I see you, but that is not
how it works.
So, I am going to take this
time to show you what you
have and, well, by the time
you would believe that you are
worth it, you would want me
anyways.

I guess I might have hurt you
more than a mighty pen does.

I guess you have not been the culprit, but somehow the winds turn their turn and bring up stories of the days of which I am not concerned.

Affection is the greatest bias of all.

His was the only name that shone brighter than the stars. The only traits that could not be neglected, the only actions that had no resemblance with others.
His spirit was the kind that shone bright in nights of despair.

You and I here have waited so long for this to come true, but

it no more feels like the desire
captivates us anymore.
Like the veins of its passion are
long gone and long hidden.

I do not even realize why you
are there.
Why would you want to be?
Why would anyone want to be
at a place where nothing ever
returns once it flows down in
the drain of ashes to be gone
forever?
Where nothing is kept for
sure.
And presumptions change like
the moon.

You rise like the bleak points
of an arrow, stretching just as
far as you could,
Just as far as you should,

And you may tear things that
possess no substance, apart
But it is all about your
conscience and my heart.

I like how my heart sinks at
the sound of losing you,
How even intoxication cannot
help it,
How it becomes an irony,
The fact that what you need
the most is taken at the most
potential moments.

And maybe it is for my own
good that no one else can see
how beautiful a soul you are!
How intricate your movements
feel, how underestimated your

actions are seen to be, And how unidentified your efforts go.

You have been such a part that it has become impossible for my life to flow its flow without you.

We are all afraid to let someone touch our heart, for we all know the damage it could do as time moves.
Because we hold our hearts in a place so close to our sanity that if it were gone, we would be left with nothing.

I would love to teach you how it is done, but in order to do that, I need to set the tresses in my soul straight first.

PSYCHE

One always needs to have a track of what is happening deep inside his soul, more than he needs to know what the world is up to.

Maybe we all fail real bad for once in our lives.
I guess once is allowed.

I do not want to be remembered as a pretty person,
A dry soul instead,
A rigid heart, maybe a kind conscience,
An open mind,

A confused train of thought,
An intellectual who does not
know when to stop,
A heartbroken soul that smiles,
A poet who can't help but
rhyme,
A child who does not believe
in pain,
A traveller whose walks have
never gone in vain,
A lover who will never love
again.

The bearing of it becomes
bearable when you know the
cause of it.

Things would not have been
touching our hearts if art was
that mediocre a concept.

One of the most beautiful paths are where you steer clear of your inhibitions.
Where what could have been does not bother.
Where what will be made to happen possesses the raw strength.

I have come way too ahead to bear a heartache again when you throw me away into a world of my past.

It is only the gods that know of your struggles - and gods do not exist.

If we all take a minute out and ask ourselves as to what it is that stops us from loving our own selves, we would probably realize that the answer we receive is way too weak than the strength we possess.

The future can certainly be cherished without being entirely aware of it.

Since there is no one perfect being, we are all just versions of each other.

We are like minute creatures in front of the moon. We are all like things competing for honours larger than our lives.

There are things that look the most beautiful in the minimal value they are supposed to be in.

The absence of colour brings a new horizon altogether,
You put in whatever you feel,
You look at whatever that pleases,
And keep with yourself whatever you want.

Maybe the real beauty of life comes with the heartaches.
Maybe a simple life does not do justice to the ethereal concept of being alive.

And you are still not sure
about who you are. You may
never be.
You are yet to search for what
consists of you.

Maybe we will all end up
feeling the same way for the
rest of our life feeding our
dreams until the end of time
comes.

We let clothes cover us. We
let the inhibitions and plastic
faces that come with them
cover us.
We become our clothes.
While all that we are beneath
it is the same.
All that hurts us is the same.

We are all maybe just vulnerable souls shielding ourselves against things we create.

Pour your potential out to the world.
 It needs it more than you do.

Go out there.
Create it. Create what you do not have.
Build up what has not been given to you.
Find what you have been longing for.

Let your soul be free. Let it take you places you did not know existed. Let it help you

find yourself. Let it travel to places.
Do not judge.
Do not stop.
Let go.

The fact that you are reading this right now signifies that you are alive.
It readily means that at this moment you can be who you want to be. Period.

Sometimes it is in the lost paths where one finds himself.

What hypocrites we are for noticing thoroughly how

pleased others are but failing to work on our own possibilities.

Drown me in my dreams,
there may not be a tomorrow,
be it anything else,
but no one wants to die of sorrow.

It is easy to think that it is not made for you or that you are not made for it - but had it been that way, you would have already been lucky enough to experience it.
You did not. It made you wait. The moment made you wait. It wanted for the right time to come. It wanted for you to open the door for it and now

that its time has come, it is
here.
Right before you.
Hoping you would believe it.

Hold on pretty heart, the
strength will pay.

Give life another chance.
Give yourself another chance.
Allow yourself to be happy.
Forgive yourself and move
ahead.
It is a short life after all, and
trust me,
It does not wait for you.

Once you start taking steps to
help yourself, you do not need
to compare your progress with
others.

Once you are done with it, you'll know why.

That is, maybe the beauty of life. We want things and we cannot have them. We want things that we cannot have.
We are pre occupied with feelings that seem to feel real. We are lost with feelings that do not have an impact.

Tonight I feel things more blurred than before,
I feel more fear in things I do not like,
I feel more pain in things that I fear,
So it all may be a wrap up?

A wrap up for the things I have
been hiding,
Things I have given up on?
Things I have been putting off
for no reason.

I have been here before,
At this very point,
Feeling this very feeling
And yet it doesn't stop me
from feeling as miserable as it
had been back then.

We do not realize how
beautiful we become until we
start loving ourselves.

It starts at the deepest of the
nights,

When the moon is at its
shiniest path,
And the silence is louder than
ever,
That is when life happens.

We all let go of ourselves the
day we let go of our dreams.

We are all mere creatures
trying to find our escape.
Some believe in gods.
Some believe in fate.

Life is a path.
Some days you fall.
Some days you do not walk
at all.

Then it so happens that she forgets to remind herself of the strength she possesses.
Just so she has a reason to cry herself to sleep at night.

We all have a world of our own.
What it consists of differs.
No matter where we go, no matter who we meet, our own world stays with us.

Everything you cannot control happens for a reason.

If you are not happy, nothing matters.
If you are happy, nothing else matters.

Those seemingly unimportant things that keep coming up on your mind might be your path of joy.

For anybody who is out there, trying to find reasons why it won't happen.
For anybody out there who feels that he or she is running out of blessings.
It will happen. Whatever is that you wish for - I promise you it will happen.
You do not know me, nor do I know you, but just the fact that you took your time out to read this motivates me enough to try to motivate you a little more, if you allow me so.

So, if you care enough, try giving up on why it won't happen.
If it matters enough, stop counting your setbacks.
Go out there and just do what is needed to be done.

You do not need courage for something you do not believe in.
Your mind knows already you aren't willing to succeed.

Being able to live with the potential is as crucial as building it.

Now is the time and it is never
coming back again.
You better pick up the tools
for time waits for none.
Nor does the world.

Your wishes do not submit to
the reality of life.

My belongings do not define
me, nor do my choices. I am
way more than what I let you
see, way deeper than I let
you in.

All of us are biased in favour
of the present till it becomes
our past.

No one has ever made it big with the obvious rules - but with the simple ones.

Let us all explore what has not been born and fill our souls with the illusion that awaits us.

All the broken pieces of hope become our reality.

A smile is all it takes to conveniently trick your heart into believing that everything is fine.

Let us all laugh like it was meant to be,

Deliberately forgetting what kills and unintentionally holding on to what pleases.

Weak enough to go on,
Contented enough to give up.

We are all scared more than we are living.
Scared that they will get to know.
Scared that they won't accept.
Scared that everything we hold close will break, even if it is us that exert the intense burden.
Scared that nothing may remain the same.
And more than anything that helps, it is this fear that eats up

our entire circle of existence instead.

Let us bring out our naked souls.
Let them see what we really are and,
How we hide our critical emotions.

Let me contemplate what is possible, for there are a hundred faces we all have and a million masks we all wear.

We are all maybe drunk on the idea of protecting our egos.
We are not hurt.

- Our ego is - for we use them as shields against the universe, the entire universe.

So darling, for some of us with broken hearts, our hearts aren't broken, our ego is scarred.

We all do it out of habit, hurt ourselves out of habit, expect out of habit. It is mostly when you are all alone, only with yourself that you can think straight.

Life has really made your mind and your heart wire you in such a way that is so fixed that even the enemies you have could never be your friends, but then it has provided you with such an array of emotions that the ones you love could very well become your enemies.

Every cell of my body strengthens and stretches into something I do not want to become. As every part loosens, I lose a piece of my soul to the shallow endeavours.
And I swear to an extent of no return that all I want to do is go back to where it all started.

So many traces of failure dedicated to my soul,
sometimes what feels best is to walk alone.

Another soul I do not know of,
A new set of misery waiting for me to be checked,

For it is with every person I meet,
That none of us is free from our own systems that introspect.

Well, darling, you will not be able to understand the half of me unless you are entirely drunk on the thought of hating yourself to the point of no return.

I am at my worst when nostalgia creeps in, when bouts and thoughts of what used to be, appear,
when what is not there anymore shrinks me to the emotional core.

At nights, we are all the same
all the broken pieces of us,
all the unfulfilled hopes,
all the unforgettable joys so far,
become our reality and get the
best of us.

The most beautiful things in
life hit you when you are least
expecting them.

If you take a closer look,
petrifying sadness is as good
as tranquil and thorough
sadness.

Let us try and not kill the life
in us.

I want to be a teacher for a day
or two,
a painter,
a pilot,
a dancer.
and just when I will be done
with it,
I want to realize that peace
of the soul is the common
denominator,
and it does not matter what
you put your time to as long
as it serves your mind.

Of course it is you who takes
the big steps, but sometimes it
is also the love you need.
Of course it does not matter
what they say, but the beliefs
you breed.

The best way you could ever reward yourself is by letting go of your inhibitions, by accepting yourself just the way you are.

And if there is any way you can look forward to your life, It is by forgiving yourself, by letting go of all that you feel holds you back, of all that you think you are not worthy of.

You, my love, were worthy of each and every vibe of positivity that ever came your way or ever will, no matter what they say.

DARKNESS

You are the shadow that follows
me in the dark hallways.
The pain numbness feels like.
The essence death has.
The flavour raindrops bring.
The darkness light hides.
You are like dark to me, like
nights.
The kind of moments I wait for.

It is strange what light does to
dark!
It exploits it,
Steals away it's very existence

Gives birth to something that is too different from the dark.

You do not follow your passion to make sense.

You do it because it brings your insane dark side out in the open without any

Drowning into the dark sorrow feels better than swinging between the two sides of life, not knowing which way to go.

I would kill to have you back
for I crave the dark influence
your soul had on mine.

Broken as a bird's wing,
Irrecoverable so it can't swing,
I've never had thoughts this
deep.
This is just a mirror to the
beliefs so steep.

Let us all forget the heart's
cries,
Remember the clear skies.
Forget the dark days,
Remember the warm nights.

The dark doesn't love me
enough.

It leaves me every time a bright ray of hope appears.

It was her soul that craved for the darkness.
It was her mind that demanded for darkness to be free.

Dark - for her had a charm.
She knew where she was going and still could not see it.
She knew what had her and still wasn't aware of the path she tread upon.

You are just so used to your life that you no more believe in the possibility of miracles.

As the night arrives,
I am all alone,
The touch, the fear crawls back.

I am the magic you seek in dark nights,-
covered with globules of dew,
fighting uncertainty,
for I am not visible to the craving you explore.
And life is not always going to serve you right or serve you well, for that matter.
You might as well anyways do your best to serve yourself.

The nights prove to be scary. The kind of scary they warn you about. The kind of scary that runs after your soul. The kind that does not leave you alone.

Perhaps it is these nights that finally mould you to be the kind of person that you are the next morning.

Perhaps it is these nights that disrupt you and do not let you be the person you want to be.

As the night comes closer, I only want to let go of what hurts, for you could be the one who could heal himself, but I am one of those who rather needs another soul.

What else feels pathetic than having everything it needs and yet following the path of vulnerability

Not realizing what you have
and what you could make of it.

It goes in the bloodstream,
flickering into it like it was
meant to stay.

You underestimated the time
to wait for your dreams to
come true - now you can't wait
to finally have it.

Some days, I just want to
drown in the intoxication like
that of a glass of whiskey,
and complain of things I could
not have for I did not try,

Lie down under the light of
the moon,

and stick to the anticipation of a new beginning.

It is the misery that gets the best of me.
This fear that leads to nowhere.

Let my body collide with the black sky and drain the inabilities of my soul.